Homeless But Not Hopeless

Robert (Bob) Marshall Author

Homeless But Not Hopeless

Beneath the stars, a bench my bed,

A roof of sky, where dreams have fled.

The world moves on, but here I stay,

In shadows cast by yesterday.

A stranger's smile, a hand outstretched,

Kindness found where hope was etched.

Through laughter, tears, and endless fight,

I find a spark within the night.

No home, no hearth, yet still I stand,

With fragile hope cupped in my hand.

For life may strip, but cannot take,

The will to heal, rebuild, remake.

Index

Preface

A Note on Homelessness

Reality vs Perception

Chapter 1:

Spring Chill and the Stories of Survival

Chapter 2:

Street Life—Trials, Tribulations, and Humour

Chapter 3:

Strangers and Friends—Finding Laughter in Unexpected Places

Chapter 4:

Unexpected Generosity—From Street Debates to "Luxury" Meals

Chapter 5:

Finding Solace in Friendship—Carl and I

Chapter 6:

The System That Tried (and Often Failed) to Help

Chapter 7:

Street "Innovations" and Surviving with Style

Chapter 8:

Luxury Living—Redefining "High Class"

Chapter 9:

The Weight of the Night

Chapter 10:

The Invisible Lines

Chapter 11:

Friendships Forged in the Shadows

Preface:

Homelessness is a word that conjures stark images, cold nights, cardboard beds, and the haunting shadow of despair. For those who've never experienced it, it's easy to reduce homelessness to a list of stereotypes: addiction, laziness, or simply "bad choices." The truth, as I've learned firsthand, is far more complicated. Homelessness is not just about losing a roof over your head; it's about losing a sense of place, of identity, and sometimes even the belief that you matter.

This book isn't a guide to solving homelessness, nor is it a tale of unrelenting misery. Instead, it's a story about survival, resilience, and the strange humour that emerges when you're forced to live on the edge of society. It's about the friendships that form in the unlikeliest of places, the small acts of kindness that remind you the world isn't entirely cruel, and the bureaucratic absurdities that make you laugh when crying feels inevitable.

To protect the dignity and privacy of those still living this nightmare, some individuals and incidents in this book have been fictionalised. However, the essence of their struggles and their triumphs remains authentic. It is a reflection of the reality many face and a tribute to the courage it takes to endure.

Homelessness is not a one-size-fits-all experience. For some, it's a deliberate choice—a rejection of conventional responsibilities, taxes, and societal norms. They remove themselves from the system, finding freedom in a life that others might view as chaotic or unbearable. But for many, homelessness is not a choice. It's a cruel twist of fate—a relationship gone wrong, a lost job, a sudden illness. That was my reality. I didn't choose this life; it chose me, and navigating it became a journey I never imagined I'd have to face.

This book would not be complete without recognising the incredible work being done by organisations and individuals in the Northwich area. The Salvation Army, in particular, is a lifeline for many, offering food, warmth, and compassion without judgment. Their efforts are complemented by numerous other charities, community groups, and volunteers who pour their hearts into making life a little easier for those of us on the streets.

Equally, a certain individual within Cheshire West Council went above and beyond, working tirelessly within a flawed system to offer genuine care and support. Her dedication reminds us that, while bureaucracy can fail, human kindness often succeeds. Their work is vital, and their impact is felt far beyond what can be measured. Some of their restrictions are cards dealt from the Government themselves.

The other people who have witnessed this journey and have provided support that simply can not be quantified, one a lady I've known for over forty five years and worked alongside her during my time within the Police. The other priceless person on this journey is my brother David – Thank You.

Northwich itself is a town steeped in history, known for its picturesque waterways and strong community spirit. Nestled in the heart of Cheshire, it boasts a unique charm, blending the old and the new with its timber-framed buildings and vibrant local businesses. But like any community, it has its challenges. Homelessness here isn't as visible as it might be in larger cities, but it's no less real. The town's warmth and resilience are reflected in the people who fight daily to support those who've fallen through the cracks.

As a gesture of gratitude and a way to give back, a percentage of the proceeds from this book will go directly to homeless charities in the Northwich area. These funds will support the vital work being done to provide shelter, food, and hope to those still enduring the hardships of life on the streets.

I wrote this not to inspire pity but to spark understanding. Homelessness can happen to anyone. One bad decision, one piece of bad luck, or one moment of vulnerability can change everything. But the people behind the labels—the rough sleepers, the bus station dwellers, the park bench regulars—are more than their circumstances. They're people with stories, struggles, and an incredible capacity for hope, even in the darkest times.

To those who have walked similar paths, I hope this book offers a sense of solidarity and perhaps even a smile. To those who've never faced such challenges, I hope it opens your eyes to the reality of life on the margins.

This is not just my story—it's the story of everyone who has ever been overlooked, misunderstood, or underestimated. It's proof that, even when life strips you of almost everything, the human spirit can endure, laugh, and rebuild.

Robert Marshall

Author of Homeless But Not Hopeless

A Note on Homelessness:

Reality vs Perception

Homelessness is a complex issue, far removed from the stereotypes often associated with it. Many people assume it's the result of bad choices or personal failure, but the truth is far more nuanced. Homelessness can stem from sudden life changes—job loss, relationship breakdowns, or health crises—or from systemic failures like inadequate mental health support or the lack of affordable housing. For most, it is not a choice but a devastating consequence of circumstances beyond their control.

While some individuals may choose a transient lifestyle, rejecting societal norms, they represent a small fraction of the homeless population. The majority are striving to regain stability, navigating the immense challenges of living without a home in a world that often looks away. Every person on the streets has a story—stories of resilience, struggle, and survival.

Thankfully, there are people and organisations offering hope. Charities, outreach workers, and community groups work tirelessly to provide shelter, food, and dignity to those in need. Their efforts remind us that solutions arc possible when compassion meets action.

Homelessness is not just about the loss of a roof over one's head; it's about the loss of security, identity, and connection. Addressing it requires understanding, empathy, and systemic change. Only then can we move beyond perception to truly solve the problem.

Chapter One:
Spring Chill and the Stories of Survival

Spring Chill and a Familiar Bench

Early May 2024. The calendar said spring, but the weather clearly hadn't received the memo. The chill wrapped around Northwich like an old, damp blanket, settling in the bones of anyone unfortunate enough to linger outside. On my bench at the bus station—"my bench," as I'd come to think of it—I huddled beneath layers of clothes and blankets that barely kept the cold at bay. The metal beneath me was unforgiving, biting through every barrier as if reminding me of my place in the world. The town was waking up. Shopkeepers rolled up their shutters with the weary determination of people who'd done it a thousand times before. The air was filled with the sounds of life: schoolchildren's shouts mingling with the hiss of buses and the distant whine of a street cleaner. People hurried past, heads down, clutching takeaway coffees and pulling their jackets tight. They seemed to sense the cold differently than I did; for them, it was temporary, an inconvenience. For me, it was the constant companion of another endless day.

A pigeon strutted into my field of vision, its small, greedy eyes fixed on the remains of a sandwich I'd been saving. It stopped a few feet away, cocked its head, and stared at me as if deciding whether I was worth the effort.

"You and me both, mate," I muttered, holding the sandwich a little closer. "This is all I've got today, so jog on."

The pigeon, unmoved by my threat, edged closer, its neck bobbing rhythmically. It wasn't bravery—it was confidence. This bird had lived on these streets longer than I had and probably fared better. With a resigned sigh, I tore off a corner and tossed it onto the pavement. The pigeon darted forward, snatched the offering, and flapped away in triumph. I watched it go, chuckling despite myself.

It was strange, the things you got used to. This bench, for one. I'd chosen it because it was slightly sheltered from the wind and because no one else seemed to want it. The graffiti etched into its surface—names, hearts, the occasional swear word—had become familiar, like the pages of a book I read daily. The bus station's hum, the steady flow of strangers coming and going, was the background music of my new life.

The Downward Spiral

A year ago, I couldn't have imagined living like this. Back then, I was Robert Marshall—a former police officer, a man who understood discipline, structure, and order. My life hadn't been perfect, but it had been stable. A home. A partner. A sense of purpose. Now, those things felt like distant memories, fragments of a story that belonged to someone else.

The fall didn't happen all at once. It was gradual, like watching a stone roll down a hill. First, there was the strain in my relationship, subtle cracks that I ignored for too long. Then came the war in Ukraine, something I got involved in and witnessed firsthand, compounded by my own stubborn refusal to ask for help. The final blow was an argument—one of those blistering rows where everything you've bottled up comes out in a torrent of anger and hurt. Harsh words were exchanged, doors slammed, and a few weeks later, after coming back from London. I was out of her house with nothing and no idea where to go. Deeply emotional and hard for both of us.

Homelessness wasn't something I'd ever thought about. It wasn't a possibility in my mind—not for someone like me. I'd always been the one offering help, the one stepping in when things went wrong. But life has a cruel way of reminding you that no one is immune. One moment, you're part of the crowd, and the next, you're sitting on a bench, invisible to the world around you.

Moments of Self-Reckoning

The first nights were the hardest. I remember walking aimlessly, trying to find somewhere—anywhere—that felt safe. I ended up on this bench, drawn by the faint light of the bus station and the illusion of security it offered. It wasn't home, but it was better than nothing. And nothing was the alternative.

Sitting there in the early hours, with the world around me quiet, I had plenty of time to think. Too much time. I thought about her, about the life we'd built—or rather, the life she'd built, with me as a guest who'd overstayed his welcome. I thought about the mistakes I'd made, the chances I hadn't taken to fix things before they broke beyond repair.

But mostly, I thought about my own failures. Depression wasn't new to me. It had been a shadow in my life for years, a quiet, insidious presence that I'd always managed to keep at bay. Or so I thought. Looking back, I realised how much it had shaped my decisions—or lack of them. I'd buried myself in work, convinced that staying busy would keep the darkness at arm's length. But when the work stopped, the shadow was still there, waiting.

The Breaking Point

May 2024 wasn't just the month I lost my home. It was the month I nearly lost everything. I'd reached a point where the weight of it all felt unbearable. The shame, the loneliness, the sense of being completely adrift—it was too much. One night, I drove to a quiet spot near Oulton Park, parked the car, and let the engine run. I closed my eyes and waited for the numbness to take over.

But it didn't. Fate, luck, or something more divine intervened. A passing dog walker noticed the car, stopped to check, and found me unconscious. The next thing I knew, I was in a hospital bed, surrounded by beeping machines and pitying faces.

The nurses were kind, though their concern felt like salt on an open wound. They spoke to me softly, as if I might shatter if they raised their voices. I hated it. But more than that, I hated myself for needing their help. The shame was a heavy, suffocating blanket I couldn't shake.

And yet, waking up in that hospital bed was a turning point. Not the kind you see in films, with swelling music and sudden clarity. It was quieter than that, more like a flicker of light in a dark room. I didn't want to be there, but I was. And if I was still here, maybe there was a reason.

A Former Life as a Policeman

Back on the bench, I often thought about my years on the force. Manchester in the '80s and '90s wasn't for the faint-hearted. The city had its share of violence, poverty, and heartbreak, and I'd been in the thick of it. I thought I'd seen it all—domestic disputes, armed robberies, the hollow-eyed despair of addicts, murders. I thought I understood struggle.

But homelessness was a different kind of struggle. It wasn't about quick decisions or adrenaline-fuelled moments. It was slow, grinding, relentless. It stripped away everything that made you feel human—your dignity, your identity, your sense of worth. On the streets, there were no badges, no uniforms, no authority. There was just survival.

Northwich Morning Encounters

Not everyone in Northwich looked away. There was Alan, for one. He was a wiry man in his late fifties, with a face that told a thousand stories he'd never share. Alan had spent 18 years in prison—what for, he never said, and I never asked. We sat in companionable silence most mornings, punctuated by the occasional nod or grunt. He had a knack for finding the day's crossword, even if it meant fishing it out of a bin. His determination to complete it, despite missing half the clues, was oddly inspiring.

Then there were the pigeons, who showed no such restraint. Bold, cheeky, and utterly indifferent to human struggles, they ruled the bus station with an iron beak. Watching them squabble over a dropped chip or circle an unsuspecting commuter was a strange kind of entertainment.

Meeting PC Care and Constable Comfort

The real highlights of my mornings, though, were PC Care and Constable Comfort. Unlike most people, who averted their eyes or hurried past, these two stopped. They saw us—really saw us. PC Care was bubbly and warm, her energy a welcome burst of light in a grey world. Constable Comfort, true to her name, was quieter but just as kind.

One particularly cold morning, PC Care arrived with two cups of tea and a bag of biscuits. "Morning, love," she said, handing me a steaming cup. "Can't have you turning into an icicle, can we?"

I smiled, wrapping my hands around the cup. "Feels like I'm halfway there."

Constable Comfort, always the straight man to her partner's jokes, added, "British spring—never one to keep its promises."

Alan:

Friendship and Betrayal

But the streets have a way of pulling the rug out from under you. One morning, Alan didn't show up. At first, I thought he'd moved on or found a shelter. Then the whispers started—rumours of an arrest, of charges I didn't want to believe.

The betrayal cut deep. I'd shared my mornings with this man, trusted him in a way that the streets rarely allowed. To learn that trust had been misplaced was a bitter pill to swallow.

PC Care, perceptive as ever, saw the turmoil in my face.

"Sometimes, we don't know people as well as we think," she said gently. "It's not your fault."

Lessons in Trust

Alan's betrayal made me wary, but it didn't close me off entirely. Trust was a gamble, but so was survival. And for every disappointment, there were moments of light—like PC Care's tea, Constable Comfort's quiet humour, or the simple kindness of a passer-by who offered a sandwich without judgment.

On the streets, survival wasn't just about food or warmth. It was about connection. About finding small moments of humanity in a world that often felt cold and indifferent. For all the challenges, I held onto one belief: this was not the end of my story. Not yet.

Chapter Two:

Street life—Trials, Tribulations, and the Odd Slice of Humour

---

Street Life in Northwich:

Chaos and Characters

Living on the streets of Northwich wasn't just about finding somewhere to sit or something to eat. It was a daily improvisation, a battle to carve out a shred of normality in a world that felt anything but. There were routines, sure, but the unpredictable was always lurking, ready to turn your day upside down in a moment.

Northwich wasn't London, but it had its quirks, its own bustling energy. The town was small enough that you started recognising people within days, but big enough to hide in when you needed to. Market Street, with its shops and occasional charity events, was a hub of street life. The bus station was my domain, though—my throne, if you will, complete with pigeons as my unwilling court.

Each day brought a rotating cast of regulars and strangers, all part of the street theatre. It wasn't a life I would have chosen, but it was mine now, and I was learning the rules of the game—rules nobody teaches you but that you somehow absorb, like the unspoken etiquette of where to sit, how to queue, and when to speak up or stay silent.

The Salvation Army:

A Sanctuary for the Soul

The Salvation Army became a lifeline early on. I'd resisted going at first. Pride has a way of getting in the way of common sense, even when you're sitting on a bench with damp socks and an empty stomach. But hunger eventually won the argument, and I found myself walking through the doors.

The first thing that struck me was the warmth. Not just the physical heat of the room, though that was heavenly, but the atmosphere. The volunteers greeted everyone like old friends, their smiles genuine and their words kind. They didn't ask questions that made you squirm, didn't judge you for where you'd come from or what you'd done. They just saw you as a person.

The food wasn't Michelin-starred, but it was hot, filling, and cooked with care. I remember sitting down with my first plate—a bowl of soup and a slice of bread—and feeling something I hadn't felt in weeks: a sense of relief. For that brief moment, I wasn't a man on the streets. I was just a man having a meal.

The Queue for Showers: The Great Battle

Now, you might think waiting for a shower is a mundane thing. For us, it was a ritual, a sport, and a test of character all rolled into one. There was only one shower, and it was in high demand. Getting your turn wasn't just about patience; it was about strategy.

The regulars were experts. They'd perfected the art of loitering near the door without looking like they were loitering. They'd strike up casual conversations, all while keeping one eye on the queue, ready to pounce the moment the shower was free. These were the tacticians.

Then you had the storytellers—the ones who used the queue as their stage. Dave was one of them. He'd regale us with tales of his past, most of which sounded wildly exaggerated.

"I once went two months without a shower," he announced one morning, puffing out his chest. "Lived in the woods, I did. Used to bathe in streams. You lot wouldn't last a day out there."

"Dave," Moira replied, not even looking up, "you couldn't last a day without your crisps, never mind the woods."

Then there were the queue jumpers—the bold, the brazen, and the occasionally clueless. One young lad tried it during my second week. He sauntered to the front like he'd been invited, only to be met with a chorus of disapproval.

"Oi!" Phil bellowed, his voice echoing off the walls. "Back of the queue, mate! We're not savages, but we've got rules!"

The lad shuffled away, muttering under his breath. I made a mental note: never mess with the shower queue hierarchy. It was sacred.

Respect for the Salvation Army

For all the chaos outside, there was an unspoken reverence for the Salvation Army. Even the rowdiest among us seemed to instinctively understand that this was a place of safety, dignity, and humanity. It wasn't just the volunteers who set the tone—it was the space itself. It offered warmth, not just physically but emotionally, and we all felt it.

Phil, who was never one to take life too seriously, had his own little ritual. He'd always leave his beer or cider outside before stepping through the door.

"God's watching, isn't he?" he'd say with a grin, setting down his can.

Moira, ever the realist, would roll her eyes. "If God's watching, he's probably laughing at the state of us."

Inside, the rough edges softened. Voices dropped, laughter turned gentle, and even the toughest characters showed a flicker of vulnerability. It was like we all understood, on some unspoken level, that this was a place where we could let our guard down.

Phil's Survival Tactics:

Equal Parts Genius and Ridiculous

Phil was a character and a half. A wiry bloke in his 50s, he'd only been on the streets for a few months, but he carried himself like a seasoned veteran. He'd dubbed himself a "street survivalist," though his tactics were often more laughable than effective.

Take his obsession with bakery bins, for example. Every morning, Phil would make his rounds, digging for discarded pastries like a treasure hunter. He'd return triumphantly, holding up his finds as if they were gold.

"Look at this," he said one morning, holding up a stale doughnut. "Still good as new!"

"It's green," I pointed out.

"Extra flavour," he replied, taking a bite without hesitation.

Then there was his footwear innovation: cardboard shoes. He'd run out of money for proper shoes, so he'd fashioned a pair out of cardboard and duct tape.

"Who needs Nike when you've got Phil Originals?" he said, showing them off.

"Eco-friendly," I said with a smirk. "You'll be a trendsetter."

Moira:
The Queen of the Streets

Moira was a force of nature. She'd been on the streets longer than most and had claimed the bus station as her kingdom. Her morning patrols were legendary. She'd pace up and down, barking at anyone who dared step out of line.

"Oi, Jimmy!" she shouted one morning. "Stop skulking around like a lost dog. If you've got nothing to do, go sweep the pavement!"

Jimmy, a scrawny teenager with a knack for looking guilty even when he wasn't, muttered something under his breath and shuffled off. Moira nodded, satisfied.

Despite her gruff exterior, Moira had a soft side. She'd occasionally bring me a blanket or a cup of tea, always with a grumble about how I'd "freeze to death if I didn't smarten up." It was her way of showing she cared.

The Bus Station Crew

The bus station wasn't just a place to sit. It was a community, a microcosm of humanity. There was Big Tony, a hulking figure who looked intimidating but had a voice like velvet. He'd hum Motown tunes to himself, his deep baritone adding a strange beauty to the mornings.

Then there was Linda, the "cat lady," who somehow always had at least two stray cats in tow. She'd talk to them like they were her children, scolding them for wandering off or stealing food.

"Paws, if you touch that sandwich, you'll be grounded!" she said one morning, wagging her finger at a scruffy tabby.

And, of course, there was Dennis, the conspiracy theorist, who could turn even the most mundane event into evidence of a government plot.

"Why do you think the bins are always full?" he asked one day. "It's deliberate. They want us to stay here, scavenging, so they can keep an eye on us."

"Right," Phil replied. "And the pigeons are their undercover agents, I suppose?"

Dennis didn't miss a beat. "Exactly."

A Fragile Camaraderie

For all its quirks, life on the streets had a strange camaraderie. We laughed, we argued, we shared what little we had. It wasn't the life I wanted, but it was the life I had. And in those moments—laughing at Phil's antics, listening to Tony's humming, or trading barbs with Moira—I found a sense of belonging.

It wasn't perfect. It wasn't easy. But it was ours.

Reflection

Street life was a patchwork quilt of struggles and triumphs, stitched together with scraps of humour, resilience, and humanity. For every challenge, there was a moment of levity. For every setback, there was a small victory. It was a life of contradictions, but somehow, it kept me going.

Because on the streets, survival wasn't just about enduring the cold. It was about finding warmth in the people around you, however fleeting it might be.

Chapter Three:

Strangers and Friends—Finding Laughter in Unexpected Places

Market Street:

Where Survival Meets Comedy

Market Street wasn't just a place to gather scraps of food or wait for charity workers. It was our makeshift community centre, a stage for the oddest social club you could imagine. It didn't matter how cold it was, or how much the wind tried to whip us off our feet; someone was always there, ready with a wild theory, a dodgy scheme, or a story that stretched the limits of credibility.

We didn't have much, but what we lacked in material wealth, we made up for in sheer absurdity. If surviving on the streets was an art form, Market Street was the gallery.

Dennis's Grand Conspiracies:

The Government and the Bins

Dennis was our resident theorist, though "theorist" might be too kind a word. He could take any ordinary occurrence and twist it into evidence of a sinister plot. One morning, he stood in the middle of Market Street, gesturing dramatically at the bins.

"They're tracking us!" he declared, his voice ringing out over the murmurs of early shoppers. "The council's installed cameras in the bins. They're watching what we throw away to keep tabs on us."

I couldn't help but laugh. "Dennis, if they're spying on you, they're gonna be real disappointed with your crisp packets."

Dennis ignored me, turning to a bemused couple who'd stopped to watch the spectacle. "Think about it! Why else would they empty the bins so often? It's not for hygiene—it's surveillance!"

"Right," the man muttered, pulling his partner away. "Good luck with that."

Phil, who'd been quietly rummaging through a bag of donated food, chimed in. "So, what's the plan, Dennis? Are we storming the bins? Overthrowing the council?"

Dennis didn't miss a beat. "First, we spread misinformation. Stuff the bins with fake letters, confuse the system. Then we strike."

Moira snorted. "If you start stuffing love letters in the bins, Dennis, I'm moving to the other end of town."

Eddie the Entrepreneur's Latest Venture

Eddie had been with us for a few weeks now, but in that short time, he'd already established himself as the group's self-styled businessman. He could sell snow to Eskimos—or so he claimed.

His latest "business" involved selling mismatched gloves he'd fished out of a charity donation bag. He stood on Market Street like a proper market trader, holding up a neon-green glove in one hand and a polka-dot one in the other.

"Right, folks!" he called out to passers-by. "Exclusive offer! Designer gloves, only a fiver a pair. Mismatched is the new trend, trust me."

A middle-aged woman stopped, clearly intrigued by Eddie's audacity. "A fiver? For that?"

Eddie grinned, undeterred. "Madam, these are bespoke. Unique. You won't find another pair like them."

"Good," she muttered, walking away.

Phil, never one to miss an opportunity, wandered over and plucked a glove from Eddie's stash. "I'll take this one. Got any more 'bespoke' left-handers?"

Eddie handed him a zebra-striped glove, unbothered by the teasing. "That'll be a quid. No discounts, even for mates."

Sally's Artistic Endeavours:

Chaos on the Pavement

Sally's chalk drawings were a daily fixture on Market Street, a splash of colour on otherwise grey days. She approached her work with the intensity of a true artist, crouched low to the pavement, her brow furrowed in concentration.

"What's this one, then?" I asked one afternoon, pointing to a swirl of lines that looked vaguely like a giraffe.

"It's the circle of life," Sally said, her tone as serious as a priest delivering a sermon. "The chaos of existence, balanced by the symmetry of nature."

"Looks like a squashed jellyfish," Moira muttered, flicking her cigarette onto the pavement.

"It's abstract," Sally shot back. "You wouldn't understand."

To be fair, Sally's art did brighten up the street, even if it was trampled on within hours. One day, a pedestrian stopped to admire her latest piece—a cluster of stick figures holding hands beneath a rainbow.

"Did your kid draw this?" the man asked.

Sally bristled. "No, I did. It's a social commentary on unity."

Phil smirked. "Unity? Looks like they're queuing for a shower at the Salvation Army."

PC Care and Constable Comfort Save the Day (Again)

Market Street wasn't complete without its daily visit from PC Care and Constable Comfort. The pair had become fixtures in our lives, their good humour and kindness a welcome break from the monotony. They had an uncanny knack for showing up just as things were about to go sideways.

One afternoon, Dennis had decided to "protest" the council's alleged bin surveillance by chaining himself to a lamppost. The chain, of course, was actually a piece of string he'd borrowed from Sally's chalk bag, but it didn't stop him from shouting slogans like a seasoned activist.

"Down with the council! Free the streets!" Dennis bellowed, much to the amusement of the growing crowd.

PC Care arrived just in time, her hands on her hips. "Dennis, what are you doing?"

"Making a stand," he replied, puffing out his chest. "You lot can't arrest me for protesting."

Constable Comfort raised an eyebrow. "We can't, but we might nick you for public nuisance."

"Alright, alright," Dennis muttered, untying the string. "But you mark my words—the bins will rise up!"

Phil's Gourmet Experiments Continue

Phil's culinary experiments were legendary among the Market Street crew, though not always for the right reasons. One particularly cold morning, he decided to create what he called "Street Caesar Salad," using stale bread, a bit of lettuce he'd found in a sandwich, and a sachet of ketchup.

"Presentation is key," Phil said, carefully arranging the "croutons" on a piece of cardboard. "You eat with your eyes first."

"Good thing we're not eating with our noses," Moira said, grimacing.

Phil wasn't deterred. He handed each of us a portion, insisting we taste it. To his credit, it wasn't the worst thing I'd eaten. The worst thing was probably Dennis's attempt at "pigeon stew," but we didn't talk about that.

Unexpected Kindness

Amid the chaos and comedy, there were moments that reminded us of the kindness still present in the world. Strangers would occasionally stop to chat, hand out food, or simply offer a smile.

One day, a young woman approached with a bag of sandwiches. She was nervous, her hands trembling as she handed them out.

"I just… I wanted to help," she said, her voice barely above a whisper.

The group accepted the sandwiches with genuine gratitude, even Dennis, who usually had something sarcastic to say.

"Thanks, love," Moira said, her tone softer than usual. "This means a lot."

Moments like these didn't solve everything, but they chipped away at the loneliness, the feeling that the world had turned its back on us. They reminded us that even in the darkest times, there were still good people out there.

Reflection:

Finding Light in Darkness

Market Street was a strange, chaotic, and often ridiculous place, but it was also a lifeline. The characters who gathered there—the conspiracy theorist, the artist, the entrepreneur—were more than just fellow survivors. They were friends, each contributing in their own way to the patchwork of humour, humanity, and hope that kept us going.

We didn't have much. But we had each other. And sometimes, that was enough.

Chapter Four:

Unexpected Generosity—From Street Debates to "Luxury" Meals

The Night Cold That Clung to Everything

By the time summer should have started to peek through, the cold refused to loosen its grip. June brought longer days, but the nights were still biting, as if the seasons themselves had conspired against anyone without a roof. The metal bench at the bus station felt colder than ever, and no amount of blankets or coats seemed to make a difference.

One night, as I wrapped myself in layer upon layer of donated clothing, the thought struck me: this shouldn't be happening—not in June, not to anyone.

"You'd think we'd get a break," I muttered to myself, watching my breath mist in the dim light of the bus station.

The dampness seeped into everything—your clothes, your blankets, your bones. Sleep wasn't just elusive; it was a battle. Every hour brought a new chill, a fresh reason to shift and readjust. And when you did manage to drift off, it was never deep enough to feel rested. You woke up as tired as when you lay down, the cold clinging to you like a second skin.

The mornings were no better. Even the weak sunlight that crept over the buildings couldn't cut through the lingering chill. My fingers stiffened as I tried to fold my blankets, and my knees—already worn from years of standing and walking—felt like they'd been filled with lead.

"Summer, my arse," I muttered, wincing as I stretched.

The Generosity of Strangers

Amid the physical and emotional battering, there were moments that reminded you the world wasn't completely indifferent. Strangers, often hesitant and unsure, would sometimes approach with small offerings—food, a warm drink, or even just a kind word.

One particularly dreary morning, a young couple stopped by the bus station. They didn't say much—just handed me a steaming cup of coffee and a bag with a sandwich inside. Their nervous smiles said more than their words could.

"Thank you," I said, genuinely touched.

"No worries," the man replied, glancing at the ground. "Take care."

It wasn't just the coffee or the sandwich; it was the simple act of being acknowledged, of being seen. In a world where most people passed by without so much as a glance, these small moments felt monumental.

Not every act of generosity was practical, though. One woman once handed me a brightly coloured scarf—clearly hand-knitted—despite the fact that I was already wearing two. I thanked her sincerely, of course, but couldn't resist chuckling about it later.

"Well, at least if the cold doesn't kill me, I'll die fashionable," I joked to Carl, who nodded solemnly.

"Mate, with that many scarves, you'll be mistaken for an art installation," he replied, deadpan.

Phil's "Luxury Meals"

Phil had a knack for turning the smallest gestures into grand events. After one particularly successful day of donations, he announced he'd be preparing a "fine dining experience" for the crew.

"Tonight's theme," he declared, "is 'elevated street cuisine.' Prepare to be dazzled."

The menu included a collection of slightly squashed sandwiches, a tin of baked beans, and a box of doughnuts that were stale enough to double as paperweights. Phil laid everything out on a flattened cardboard box, arranging the items with the care of a Michelin-starred chef.

"First course," he announced, gesturing to the sandwiches, "is a deconstructed ham and cheese delight. Note the artisanal squish marks."

"You mean where it got sat on?" Moira quipped, earning a round of laughter.

Next came the baked beans, served cold, because none of us had access to a stove.

"Think of it as gazpacho," Phil suggested, spooning the beans into plastic cups.

"Phil, gazpacho's supposed to be soup," I pointed out.

"Details, Bob. It's the presentation that counts."

By the time we got to the doughnuts, the laughter had reached a crescendo. Phil handed one to Moira with an exaggerated flourish.

"And for dessert: a classic confection, aged to perfection."

Moira took a bite and winced. "Aged? This thing's prehistoric."

The Disjointed Support System

For all the moments of levity, the cracks in the support system were impossible to ignore. On paper, Northwich had a network of charities, churches, and council services designed to help people like us. In practice, it was a patchwork quilt with more holes than fabric.

One day, a well-meaning council worker turned up at the bus station, clipboard in hand. She asked me the same questions I'd answered dozens of times before—name, age, how long I'd been homeless.

"You're on the list," she assured me, scribbling something down. "We'll be in touch soon."

I nodded, though I'd learned not to hold my breath. The "list" was like a mythical creature—everyone talked about it, but no one had ever seen it.

Carl, ever the philosopher, had his own take on the situation. "It's like planting seeds in concrete," he said one afternoon. "You can water it all you want, but nothing's gonna grow."

Moira was less poetic. "The system's about as useful as a chocolate teapot," she muttered, rummaging through a bag of donated toiletries. "What am I supposed to do with six toothbrushes and no bloody bathroom?"

Navigating the Soup Kitchen Circuit

Another challenge was figuring out where to find food. Different groups offered meals on different days, but there was no coordination, no central schedule. Some days, you'd find yourself with more food than you could carry; other days, you'd go hungry.

Carl dubbed it the "Soup Kitchen Circuit" and took it upon himself to create an imaginary map of the week's offerings.

"Right," he said, pointing to a non-existent chart. "Tuesdays at St. Mary's, Thursdays with the Baptists, Fridays at the Salvation Army. It's like planning a pub crawl, only sadder."

Despite the humour, the lack of organisation often left us scrambling. One week, a miscommunication meant two groups showed up on the same day, both handing out the same meal: lentil stew. By the end of the afternoon, we were practically swimming in it.

"Hope you like lentils," Phil said, holding up a cup. "Because this is our diet now."

Reflections on the Day

As the sun dipped below the rooftops, we'd gather for a final chat before retreating to our respective corners of the town. The evenings were quieter, the jokes softer, but the bond between us stronger than ever.

On one particularly clear night, as we huddled together for warmth, Carl looked up at the stars.

"Funny, isn't it?" he said. "Out here, we've got the best view in town."

"You reckon that's worth freezing for?" I asked, smirking.

Carl shrugged. "Might be. Ask me again when I've got feeling in my toes."

Homelessness was a daily grind, a relentless cycle of discomfort and uncertainty. But it was also punctuated by moments of generosity and humour—small sparks of humanity that kept the darkness at bay. The people I shared those days with weren't just fellow survivors; they were my family, my reason to keep going.

Because even in the hardest times, a kind gesture or a shared laugh could make all the difference.

Chapter Five:

Finding Solace in Friendship—Carl and I

An Unlikely Bond

Friendships forged in hardship carry a weight that most people can't imagine. They're not built on convenience or common interests but on survival, shared struggles, and the rare moments of understanding that can pierce even the darkest days. Carl and I found each other in the chaos of street life, and while we couldn't have been more different, we fit together in a way that made the days—a little easier to bear.

Carl wasn't your typical homeless man. He carried himself with a kind of quiet dignity that hinted at a life once lived far from the streets. When he spoke, it was with the calm authority of someone who'd seen enough of the world to understand it but not enough to be bitter about it. He had his quirks, of course—his gardening metaphors could rival Dennis's conspiracy theories for sheer absurdity—but beneath the eccentricity was a man with a good heart.

"I'm not much for drama," Carl told me early on. "But if we're gonna be stuck out here, we might as well make the most of it."

"And how do you propose we do that?" I asked, raising an eyebrow.

"Start with a decent cuppa," he replied, pulling out a battered Thermos. "Can't solve the world's problems on an empty stomach—or without tea."

Carl's Car and My Bench

Unlike me, who had claimed a metal bench as my home, Carl still had his car. It was an old, beat-up hatchback with a dented bonnet and a rear bumper held on with duct tape, but to Carl, it was a palace.

"Got everything I need," he said one evening, leaning against the car with a grin. "Storage, shelter, even a stereo. Luxury living, mate."

"That stereo doesn't even work," I pointed out.

"Details," he replied, waving me off. "It's the principle."

Carl's car became our unofficial headquarters. Whenever the weather turned particularly foul, he'd invite me to sit inside, where we'd share a thermos of tea and swap stories. It wasn't exactly warm, but it was better than sitting out in the open, battling the elements.

One night, as the rain lashed against the windows, Carl leaned back in the driver's seat and sighed. "Y'know, Bob, this car's seen better days, but it's still got a bit of fight left in it."

"Like us, then?" I said, smirking.

"Exactly," he replied. "Two stubborn gits refusing to give up."

Gardening Wisdom on the Streets

Carl had been a professional gardener before life took its turn. He could name every plant, tree, and weed in Northwich, and he had a knack for finding beauty in places most people overlooked.

"See that crack in the pavement?" he asked me one morning, pointing to a small sprig of greenery poking through the concrete. "That's nature saying, 'Sod you, world, I'm growing anyway.'"

"You're comparing us to weeds again, aren't you?" I said, shaking my head.

"Not weeds," Carl corrected. "Survivors."

Carl's gardening metaphors became a staple of our conversations. He saw lessons in everything—how dandelions thrived in poor soil, how ivy could cling to even the roughest surfaces, how dead plants could enrich the ground for new growth. It was both ridiculous and strangely comforting.

"Life's like a garden," he told me one afternoon. "Sometimes you're blooming, sometimes you're being pruned, and sometimes... well, sometimes you're just fertiliser."

The Salvation Army Decision

It was Carl's idea to start volunteering at the Salvation Army. At first, I thought he was joking. After all, we were the ones relying on their help—what could we possibly offer in return?

"Perspective," Carl said simply. "We've been out here, Bob. We know what it's like. Maybe we can help someone else."

And so, one damp morning, we turned up early and offered to lend a hand. The staff, a mix of weary veterans and cheerful volunteers, welcomed us without hesitation. Carl was put to work fixing a broken chair, while I was handed a cloth and told to wipe down the tables.

It felt strange at first—being on the other side of things. But as the morning wore on, I found myself settling into the rhythm of it. The faces that came through the door were a mix of familiar and new, each carrying their own burdens, their own stories.

"You alright, mate?" I asked one man as I handed him a cup of tea.

He nodded, his hands shaking slightly as he took the cup. "Better now," he murmured.

It was a small moment, but it stayed with me. For the first time in a long time, I felt like I was doing something meaningful—something that mattered.

The Coffee Club

Carl, ever the innovator, decided to start a "Coffee Club" as a way to inject a bit of normality into our otherwise unpredictable days. Once a week, he'd scrape together enough change to buy the largest coffee he could find from the local Costa. Then he'd return to the bus station, where the crew would gather for their weekly dose of civilisation.

"Take a sip, Bob," he said, handing me the cup one morning. "That's not just coffee—it's culture."

"Culture tastes a lot like burnt beans," I replied, grinning.

The ritual became a highlight of our week. Each person took their turn with the cup, sipping it like it was fine wine and offering absurdly over-the-top critiques.

"Notes of cardboard," Moira declared one day, swirling the coffee in its paper cup. "With a hint of... is that desperation?"

"It's earthy," Dennis added, nodding sagely. "Very grounded."

Despite the jokes, the Coffee Club was more than just a chance to laugh. It was a moment of connection, a brief reprieve from the chaos of our lives.

The DIY Philosophy

Carl had a philosophy about surviving homelessness: "If you can't fix it, repurpose it."

This mantra applied to everything from food to clothing to the odd bits of rubbish we found on our walks. One day, Carl spotted an old umbrella sticking out of a bin. It was missing half its spokes and looked like it had lost a fight with a tornado, but Carl saw potential.

"With a bit of duct tape," he said, holding it up, "this could be a proper rain shield."

"You mean an improper rain shield," I corrected.

Undeterred, Carl spent the better part of an hour tinkering with the umbrella, using bits of string and tape to patch it up. When he was finished, he proudly held it over his head.

"See? Good as new."

The wind immediately caught it, flipping it inside out. Carl, ever the optimist, shrugged. "Well, it's aerodynamic now."

Serious Moments:

The Weight of It All

For all the laughter, there were moments when the weight of our situation pressed down hard. Late at night, when the bus station was quiet and the temperature dropped, the humour faded, leaving only the stark reality of where we were.

"Do you ever think about how we got here?" I asked Carl one evening, as we sat in his car, watching the rain streak down the windshield.

"Every day," he replied. "But thinking about it won't change it. The only thing we can do is keep going."

Carl's resilience was remarkable, but even he had his limits. There were days when he'd grow quiet, retreating into himself. On those days, I'd try to lift his spirits with a joke or a story, just as he'd done for me so many times before.

"You're like that stubborn weed, Carl," I told him one night. "No matter what happens, you just keep growing."

"And you're like a dandelion," he replied, smirking. "Annoying but surprisingly hard to get rid of."

Carl and I didn't have much—not in the traditional sense. But we had friendship, and in a world that often felt cold and indifferent, that was enough. We didn't solve the world's problems, and we certainly didn't solve our own, but we faced them together, one day—and one cup of coffee—at a time.

Because sometimes, surviving isn't about finding answers. It's about finding someone who'll sit with you in the chaos and remind you that you're not alone.

Chapter Six:

The System That Tried (and Often Failed) to Help

The Patchwork Quilt of Support

I touched on this earlier but if there's one thing I learned during my time on the streets, it's that the system designed to help people like me was more of a patchwork quilt than a safety net. And not the cosy, handmade kind of quilt—more like one stitched together in the dark by someone who'd never held a needle before. Everyone meant well, of course, but the disjointed nature of the services made it feel like you were running in circles, chasing a solution that never quite arrived.

Each day brought a new "official" to speak to, a new form to fill out, and a new promise that help was just around the corner. But somehow, that corner seemed to keep moving further away.

The Infamous Housing List

The most elusive creature in the system was the mythical "Housing List." It was talked about in hushed tones, always mentioned with a reassuring smile, but no one seemed to know where it actually lived. According to every worker I spoke to, I was definitely "on the list." Where exactly on the list? That was anyone's guess.

One housing officer turned up at the bus station one morning, clipboard in hand and a look of polite sympathy on her face.

"You're on the list," she assured me, jotting something down. "We're just waiting for a place to open up."

"Any idea when that might be?" I asked.

She hesitated. "It's hard to say. Could be a week, could be… longer."

"Define 'longer,'" I pressed.

"Um, well, we're doing our best," she replied, avoiding my gaze.

After she left, I turned to Carl, who was sitting on the bench beside me, munching on a slightly stale sandwich.

"What do you reckon, Carl? Think I'll have a flat by Christmas?"

"Christmas of which year?" he replied, deadpan.

Moira's Take on the System

Moira, ever the cynic, had a knack for cutting through the nonsense with her blunt observations. After one particularly frustrating encounter with a council worker, she lit a cigarette and muttered, "They've got more lists than Argos and fewer results than a dodgy SATNAV."

Another time, she showed up with a bag of donated toiletries from a charity van. Dumping the contents on the bench, she held up two toothbrushes and a bottle of bubble bath.

"Bubble bath?" she said, her voice dripping with sarcasm. "Where am I supposed to use this? The River Weaver?"

Phil, who'd been rummaging through the bag for anything useful, grinned. "Might as well. Just don't invite the ducks—they'll nick your soap."

The Soup Kitchen Circuit:

Feast or Famine

Food was another area where the system's inefficiencies shone. Northwich had a network of soup kitchens and food banks, but their schedules were about as predictable as the British weather. Some days, you'd have five different groups handing out meals, and others, there'd be nothing.

Carl, ever the strategist, tried to map out a schedule for us. "Right," he said one morning, using a stick to draw on the dirt. "St. Mary's on Tuesdays, the Salvation Army on Fridays, and… well, the rest is a guessing game."

The lack of coordination often led to bizarre scenarios. One memorable Tuesday, three separate groups turned up at the same spot, all offering lentil stew. By the end of the day, we had enough leftovers to feed half of Northwich—or at least, half the pigeons in the town centre.

Dennis, never one to miss an opportunity, decided to experiment with the surplus.

"Lentil stew pancakes," he announced, flipping a particularly thick portion onto a piece of cardboard. "Gourmet street food."

"More like gourmet street glue," Moira muttered, poking at the pancake with a fork.

PC Care's Frustrations

Even PC Care, who'd become something of an ally to us, couldn't hide her frustration with the system. One afternoon, she turned up with her usual cheerful smile, but it quickly faded as she sat down beside me.

"Do you know how many times I've reported the same people to the council?" she asked, shaking her head. "They keep telling me they'll 'look into it.' Meanwhile, you lot are still out here."

"It's like gardening," Carl chimed in. "If you don't actually pull the weeds, they just keep coming back."

PC Care smirked. "That's an interesting analogy, Carl. Though I think the council's more likely to plant weeds than pull them."

She stayed for a while, venting about the red tape that tied her hands and the policies that seemed designed to create more problems than they solved. It was oddly comforting to know that even someone on the "inside" saw the flaws as clearly as we did.

The Charity Maze

Charities, bless them, were often just as disorganised as the official services. Each group had its own niche—some focused on food, others on clothing, and others on hygiene kits—but they rarely communicated with each other. The result? Redundancy in some areas and glaring gaps in others.

One week, Carl and I ended up with four blankets each, courtesy of three different groups. While the extra warmth was appreciated, there was only so much we could carry.

"Reckon we could start our own shop?" Carl joked, holding up a particularly garish pink blanket. "Bob and Carl's Blanket Emporium."

"Or build a fort," I suggested. "Might be more fun."

On the flip side, there were weeks when we desperately needed practical items, like socks or gloves, and none seemed to be available. It was a constant juggling act, trying to make the most of what we were given while preparing for the inevitable gaps.

Moira's Commentary on Toiletries

Toiletries, in particular, seemed to be the charities' go-to offering, despite the fact that most of us didn't have access to showers. Moira once dumped out a bag of donations and held up a bottle of shampoo with a bemused expression.

"Shampoo?" she said. "For what hair? Half of us haven't seen a shower in weeks."

Phil, ever the joker, grabbed a bar of soap and sniffed it theatrically. "Ah, the scent of irony. My favourite."

Moments of Frustration and Laughter

For all its flaws, the system wasn't entirely useless. There were moments—rare but real—when everything came together, and you felt like progress might actually be possible. Like the day a local charity worker turned up with not just food but a list of practical advice on accessing housing services.

"It's not much," she admitted, handing me a leaflet. "But it's a start."

It wasn't a miracle cure, but it was something—a glimmer of hope in an otherwise bleak landscape.

Of course, there were still plenty of moments that bordered on absurdity. One day, a charity group handed out mini sewing kits. Carl, ever the optimist, pocketed his immediately.

"You laugh now," he told me, "but one day, this'll save my trousers."

"Or your dignity," I replied, smirking.

The system may have been broken, but it wasn't beyond hope. It was held together by people—volunteers, council workers, and strangers—who genuinely wanted to make a difference, even if they didn't always know how. And in those moments of kindness, those flashes of humanity, you found the strength to keep going.

Because at the end of the day, survival wasn't just about navigating the system. It was about finding humour in the absurd, friendship in the struggle, and hope in the smallest of gestures.

Chapter Seven:

Street "Innovations" and Surviving with Style

Homelessness forces you into a state of constant creativity. You learn to see potential in what others would dismiss as rubbish, finding ways to use discarded items for warmth, comfort, or even a laugh. When resources are scarce, the simplest things—a broken umbrella, a spare bit of cardboard—take on new importance. While the situation was undeniably tough, our ability to find humour in these improvised solutions made the harshness a little more bearable.

In this chapter, I'll delve into the ways we turned scraps into survival tools and how laughter became just as vital as warmth on those long, cold nights.

The Bench Becomes a Kingdom

I'd claimed a particular bench at the Northwich bus station as my own, and it quickly became more than a resting spot—it became my kingdom. Every morning, I'd sit there and survey my domain, which consisted of the other benches, a couple of litter bins, and a stubborn colony of pigeons that had clearly decided they were paying no rent.

Phil, ever the joker, dubbed me "The Bench King," and before long, the title stuck.

"Your Majesty," Moira greeted me one morning, mock-bowing. "Might we have an edict on how to keep the pigeons from stealing our breakfast?"

"Of course," I replied, adopting a royal tone. "Henceforth, all pigeons must pay a crust tax. One slice of bread per loaf consumed."

"They'll pay about as much as the council does," Dennis added, shaking his head.

Even Carl got into the spirit of things, carving a "royal crest" into a piece of cardboard with a penknife. It was a crude drawing of a pigeon wearing a crown, surrounded by an assortment of items we'd scavenged: a tin can, a sock, and what appeared to be a biscuit.

"There you go, Bob," Carl said, handing it to me. "Fit for a king."

Dennis's Pigeon Wars

Dennis took the idea of my royal edict a bit too seriously. Armed with an old crisp packet that he claimed could double as a "pigeon deterrent," he patrolled the bus station like a sentry, waving it in the air whenever one of the birds got too close.

"Oi, you! No loitering!" he yelled at a particularly fat pigeon one afternoon.

The pigeon, unbothered, continued pecking at a chip.

Dennis crinkled the crisp packet louder. "Don't make me escalate this!"

The pigeon finally fluttered away, but Dennis turned to us with a serious expression. "See? Fear is a universal language."

"You think the pigeons are afraid of you, Dennis?" Moira asked, raising an eyebrow. "They're just bored."

Despite the ribbing, Dennis persisted with his "pigeon patrol," adding to his arsenal with a bent coat hanger he claimed was a "mobile defence unit." It didn't seem to deter the birds much, but it kept the rest of us entertained.

The Invention of the "VIP Lounge"

It was Dennis again who decided we needed a place to "relax in style." Behind the bus station was a small alcove, mostly used by smokers and the occasional stray cat, but Dennis saw potential. Armed with a pile of cardboard and a few old blankets, he declared it the "VIP Lounge."

"Membership is exclusive," he announced one evening, gesturing to the makeshift seating he'd arranged. "Only the finest citizens of Northwich are welcome."

"What's the entry fee?" I asked, playing along.

"Something posh," Dennis replied. "A fancy hat, maybe. Or a chocolate biscuit."

Phil, never one to pass up a joke, handed Dennis a battered thermos. "Here you go. Vintage coffee holder. Worth at least a tenner."

Dennis inspected the thermos with exaggerated seriousness. "You're in."

The VIP Lounge became a nightly gathering spot, where we'd sit and share stories, bundled in mismatched blankets. One evening, Phil brought a stub of a candle, sticking it into an old jam jar for "mood lighting."

"Don't set the whole lounge on fire," Moira warned, eyeing the flame.

"Relax," Phil replied. "This is ambiance. Very classy."

Inspector Gadget's Masterpieces

Inspector Gadget, as we'd nicknamed him, had a knack for turning rubbish into "tools of survival." His inventions were equal parts absurd and ingenious, and they never failed to make us laugh.

"Check this out," he said one morning, holding up a spoon taped to a stick. "Multi-tool. It's a ladle, a back scratcher, and a weapon all in one."

"Or just a spoon on a stick," Moira replied, unimpressed.

Next came the "universal key," which was just an old bike lock key he'd found on the ground. According to Gadget, it could "unlock the secrets of the universe."

"Or just your old bike," Phil muttered.

The Charity Raffle

One particularly slow day, Dennis decided to liven things up by organising a "charity raffle." Each of us contributed a random item from our collections—an old sock, a bent spoon, even an empty tin of beans—and Dennis made a big show of setting up a makeshift table for the event.

"Step right up!" he announced. "Tickets are two buttons or one stale crust of bread. Big prizes await!"

Phil won the sock and immediately turned it into a puppet, making it sing a rendition of Twinkle, Twinkle, Little Star in a ridiculous falsetto. Moira won the spoon and declared it "the most useful thing I've owned in months."

By the end of the raffle, we were all in stitches, laughing so hard that even the pigeons seemed curious about the commotion.

Serious Moments Among the Chaos

For all the laughter, there were moments when the weight of our situation hit hard. Late at night, when the bus station emptied out and the cold seeped into our bones, the jokes faded, leaving only the harsh reality of where we were.

"It's not right, is it?" Carl said one evening, as I sat huddled under a blanket. "That we have to be this clever just to get through the day."

"No, it's not," I replied. "But what else can we do?"

Carl sighed. "Keep going, I suppose. And keep laughing.

The innovations we came up with may have been born of necessity, but they were also a testament to our resilience. Each invention, each joke, each shared laugh was a way of saying, "We're still here. We're still fighting."

Because in the end, survival wasn't just about keeping warm or finding food. It was about holding onto the parts of ourselves that made life worth living—our creativity, our humour, and our connection. And that, more than anything, kept us going.

Chapter Eight:

Luxury Living—Redefining "High Class"

Luxury is a relative concept. On the streets, it wasn't about gold-plated taps or plush carpets. Luxury was a dry pair of socks, a warm cup of tea, or a rare moment of quiet where you could breathe without thinking about survival. Despite the harshness, our little community had a knack for turning scraps into comfort and misery into laughter.

This chapter dives deeper into the highs and lows of street "luxury," brimming with absurd anecdotes and the humour we used to shield ourselves from the serious realities of homelessness.

Phil's Champagne Flutes:

The Return of the Aristocrats

Phil's champagne flutes became something of a mascot for our group. One rainy afternoon, he decided it was time to elevate our "lifestyle" even further. He turned up with a battered tea tray he'd found behind a café, balancing it precariously on one hand like a waiter in a fancy restaurant.

"Afternoon tea, anyone?" he asked, setting the tray down on a cardboard box.

"What's on the menu?" Moira asked, already sceptical.

"Only the finest," Phil replied. "A selection of premium biscuits—by which I mean, the broken ones they throw out—and a choice of beverages: water or, if you're feeling adventurous, watered-down cola."

We all played along, holding our champagne flutes as if we were royalty. Moira extended her pinky finger as she sipped her flat cola. "Darling, this vintage is simply divine."

Dennis joined in, inspecting a broken custard cream with exaggerated seriousness. "The texture is bold, the flavour daring. It speaks of... disappointment."

Even Carl got into the spirit, offering to "top up" everyone's drinks from a battered thermos.

For that afternoon, we weren't just surviving—we were thriving, in the silliest, most ridiculous way imaginable.

Dennis's Pigeon Strategy v2.0

Dennis's feud with the pigeons escalated dramatically when he decided to take his pigeon deterrent strategy to the next level. One morning, he showed up with a broken umbrella he'd rigged up with duct tape and string, claiming it was a "multi-purpose pigeon deterrent."

"You open it like this," he demonstrated, popping the umbrella open with a loud snap, "and the noise scares them off."

It worked—for about ten seconds. A particularly brave pigeon landed directly on top of the umbrella, staring at Dennis as if to say, "Is that all you've got?"

"Right," Dennis muttered, waving the umbrella. "Plan B."

Plan B turned out to be a loaf of stale bread he'd found, which he threw at the pigeons like a grenade. They scattered briefly but returned moments later, pecking at the crumbs with renewed enthusiasm.

"Well done, Dennis," Moira said dryly. "You've just invited them to an all-you-can-eat buffet."

Carl's Quest for the Perfect Pillow

For Carl, the ultimate luxury wasn't food or drink—it was a decent pillow. He'd been sleeping with his head propped up on an old rucksack for weeks, and it was starting to take its toll.

"One of these days," he said, rubbing his neck, "I'm going to find the perfect pillow. Something soft, supportive... a cloud for my head."

"Good luck with that," I replied. "Unless you're planning to mug the Salvation Army for their cushions."

But Carl was determined. Over the next few days, he tried everything: a bundle of old clothes, a pile of newspapers, even a squashed loaf of bread.

"It's got potential," he said, lying back on the bread pillow. "Bit lumpy, though."

Finally, he struck gold—or rather, foam. Someone left a discarded cushion near the bins, and Carl swooped in like a hawk.

"This is it," he declared, cradling the cushion like a newborn. "The dream pillow."

Of course, the dream lasted exactly two days before it started to rain, and the cushion turned into a soggy mess. Still, for those two glorious nights, Carl slept like royalty.

The "Soup Kitchen Olympics"

One of the more absurd aspects of street life was the unspoken competition between soup kitchens. Each group had its signature dish, and we'd often debate which one was the best.

"St. Mary's does a mean vegetable soup," Phil said one evening. "Thick enough to stand your spoon up in."

"Yeah, but the Baptists give out bread rolls," Carl countered. "Proper bread rolls, not those crumbly ones that disintegrate when you dip them."

The debates reached their peak one rainy afternoon when Dennis declared, "We should host a taste test. An Olympic-style ranking of soups."

And so, the "Soup Kitchen Olympics" were born. Armed with donated plastic spoons, we made our rounds, rating each soup on flavour, texture, and overall "slurpability."

"St. Mary's gets a solid eight," Moira said, sipping thoughtfully. "But points deducted for lack of seasoning."

"The Salvation Army's got heart," Carl added, "but their lentil soup is a bit... gritty."

The Olympics became a running joke, and while the competition was light-hearted, it also highlighted how dependent we were on these services. Each ladle of soup was a reminder that, for all our humour, this was survival—not a game.

Moira's Blanket Empire

If Carl was obsessed with pillows, Moira had a thing for blankets. Over the months, she'd amassed an impressive collection, thanks to charity vans and well-meaning volunteers. Her "empire" consisted of everything from scratchy woollen throws to gaudy fleece blankets with questionable patterns.

"This one's my summer blanket," she said one evening, holding up a thin, floral-print number. "Lightweight, breathable. Perfect for those balmy seven-degree nights."

"And this?" I asked, pointing to a massive, tartan monstrosity.

"Winter," she replied. "Double-layered. Practically bulletproof."

Despite the jokes, Moira's blankets were a godsend on cold nights, and she often shared them with the rest of us. Still, she couldn't resist poking fun at her own collection.

"If I ever get housed," she said, "I'm turning these into curtains. Might as well make use of them."

The Humour in Hardship

For all the laughs, there were moments when the absurdity of our situation hit hard. One evening, as we sat in Dennis's "Luxury Suite," the fairy lights casting a soft glow, Carl sighed and said, "Y'know, it's mad. We've got nothing, but we're still finding ways to laugh."

"It's either that or cry," Moira replied.

"True," I said. "But crying doesn't keep you warm."

The humour we clung to wasn't just a coping mechanism—it was a lifeline. It reminded us that we were more than our circumstances, that we still had something no one could take away: our ability to find joy, however small, in the most unexpected places.

More Unexpected Kindness

Every so often, the world would surprise us with a moment of genuine kindness. One afternoon, a woman stopped by the bus station and handed us a box of pastries from a local bakery.

"They're fresh," she said, smiling. "Thought you might like them."

For a moment, we were too stunned to respond. Then Phil broke the silence.

"Fresh pastries?" he said, his eyes wide. "Who are you, and where have you been all my life?"

The pastries were a rare treat, and we savoured every bite. But it wasn't just the food—it was the gesture itself, the reminder that, even in the harshest of circumstances, there were people who cared.

Luxury living on the streets wasn't about material wealth—it was about making the best of what you had, no matter how little that was. It was about turning soup into a competition, blankets into an empire, and broken champagne flutes into a symbol of resilience. Most importantly, it was about finding laughter in the darkest moments and holding onto the hope that, one day, things would get better.

Because if we could find joy in flat cola and stale bread, imagine what we could do with a proper roof over our heads.

Chapter Nine:

The Weight of the Night

Nights on the streets weren't just hours of darkness; they were the hardest parts of being homeless. They were long, cold, and full of both physical discomfort and mental torment. When the bustle of the day faded and the laughter of our group scattered to individual corners, the night settled in with an oppressive silence that was heavy with loneliness and fear. It wasn't just about surviving the elements—it was about enduring the raw, unfiltered weight of being utterly vulnerable in a world that seemed to have forgotten you.

The Stillness of Midnight

There's a moment, usually around midnight, when the town seemed to hold its breath. The shops were shuttered, the streets emptied, and the world became unnervingly still. It wasn't peace—it was isolation. The silence didn't comfort; it pressed down on you, amplifying the sound of your own thoughts until they became deafening.

The bench where I spent my nights felt harder and colder under the cover of darkness. During the day, it was my perch, my throne, my community spot. At night, it became a place of exile. The streetlight above flickered occasionally, casting long shadows that seemed to shift and move in ways they shouldn't. I'd tell myself it was just my tired mind playing tricks, but that didn't stop my heart from racing.

I remember one night when a cat appeared, sleek and black, with eyes like tiny golden moons. It padded silently across the pavement and paused to stare at me.

"What do you want?" I whispered. "You're not here to keep me company, are you?"

The cat tilted its head, as if weighing my words, then vanished into the shadows. I chuckled softly, despite myself. "Guess not."

The Cold's Cruel Grip

The cold at night was a different beast from the cold during the day. It wasn't just an inconvenience; it was a predator, stalking you relentlessly. Even with layers of blankets, jackets, and cardboard, it found its way in, seeping into your bones and stealing what little warmth you had left.

One particularly brutal night, frost coated every surface around me. My breath came out in clouds, and my fingers felt like they belonged to someone else—someone frozen solid. I tried everything to keep warm. I wrapped my feet in plastic bags, pulled my coat tighter, even attempted to huddle into a ball to conserve heat. Nothing worked.

By morning, I was so stiff I could barely stand. Carl found me shuffling around like an old man.

"You alright, Bob?" he asked, his face lined with concern.

"Never better," I lied, teeth chattering so hard I could barely form the words.

He handed me a cup of tea he'd scrounged from somewhere. "Here. This'll help."

It was lukewarm at best, but in that moment, it felt like the nectar of the gods.

The Visitors of the Night

Nights were never entirely quiet. While the respectable folks of Northwich were tucked up in bed, the streets came alive with their own strange cast of characters. Drunks stumbled out of pubs, their laughter echoing eerily in the emptiness. Some were friendly enough, stopping to share a joke or a story. Others were less welcome.

One night, a group of teenagers decided it would be fun to throw fast food at me. Chips, burgers, even a half-full cup of Coke—all of it came raining down while they laughed and shouted insults.

"Oi, you missed a spot!" I shouted back, trying to maintain some dignity as I brushed ketchup off my blanket.

Another time, a man with wild hair and an even wilder look in his eyes approached me, muttering about aliens.

"They're everywhere," he said, leaning in conspiratorially. "Watching us. Watching you."

"Tell them I said hi," I replied, hoping he'd move on. He didn't.

Instead, he squatted next to me and began drawing incomprehensible shapes on the pavement with a stick. "This is their language," he explained. "They talk through symbols."

I nodded, playing along. "Fascinating."

He eventually wandered off, leaving me to wonder if he was mad, or if he knew something I didn't.

Fear in the Shadows

The streets at night weren't just lonely—they were dangerous. You were exposed, vulnerable, and always on edge. Every noise—a footstep, a rustle of leaves, the distant roar of an engine—sent a jolt of adrenaline through me.

One night, I woke to find a man standing over me, his face hidden in shadow.

"Got a light?" he asked.

"No," I replied, heart pounding.

He stood there for a moment too long, his presence menacing. Finally, he muttered something under his breath and walked away, leaving me shaken and wide awake for the rest of the night.

After that, I started sleeping with my bag tucked under my head and a sturdy stick within reach. It wasn't much, but it gave me a sliver of security.

The Small Kindnesses

For all the fear and discomfort, the nights occasionally offered glimpses of humanity that kept me going. Like the time a bakery worker left a bag of day-old pastries on the bench beside me with a note that simply said, Stay safe. Or the time an older man, bundled in a coat that looked like it had seen better decades, stopped to hand me a thermos of soup.

"Don't drink it all at once," he said with a wink. "It's got to last."

I didn't know his name, and I never saw him again, but that thermos was a lifeline on more than one cold night.

Battling Myself

The hardest battles at night weren't with the cold or the drunks—they were with myself. When the world went quiet, my mind grew loud. Every regret, every mistake, every missed opportunity replayed on a loop. I'd lie awake, staring at the stars or the underside of the streetlight, wondering how I'd ended up here.

"Should've done better," I'd mutter to myself. "Should've been better."

But the self-blame didn't help. It just added to the weight of the night, pressing down on me until it felt like I couldn't breathe. On the worst nights, I wondered if it was worth it—if the fight to survive was one I even wanted to win.

The Beauty of Dawn

And then, just when it felt like the night would never end, dawn would creep over the horizon. The first rays of sunlight turned the frost to glitter, the shadows to gold. It wasn't warm, not really, but it was a promise: you made it through.

The streets began to stir, the sounds of life returning. Cars rumbled, shop shutters clattered open, and the smell of baking bread wafted through the air. The world came back to life, and so did I.

For a little while, the weight lifted. The night was over, and a new day had begun.

Nights on the streets were a test of endurance, both physical and emotional. They stripped you down to your barest self, exposing every vulnerability. But they also taught me the value of small kindnesses, of resilience, of finding light even in the darkest hours.

Because no matter how heavy the night felt, dawn always came. And as long as it did, I knew I could keep going.

Chapter Ten:

The Invisible Lines

Life on the streets was a labyrinth of invisible lines, dictating every aspect of our existence. These lines weren't painted on pavements or marked with signs, yet they controlled where we could sit, where we could sleep, and what scraps of dignity we could cling to. Some lines were drawn by authorities, others by society, and the most punishing ones were drawn in our own minds. Every day was a balancing act—straddling survival and humanity, humour and heartbreak, all while trying not to lose ourselves completely.

The Sacred Queue

Queues weren't just lines; they were the unspoken currency of the homeless community. If you wanted anything—a meal, a blanket, or even just a kind word—you had to queue for it. But queues were also fragile ecosystems, prone to collapse at the slightest provocation.

One evening, word got out about a pop-up kitchen serving shepherd's pie. The promise of actual meat (or something close to it) caused a frenzy. By the time we arrived, the queue stretched down the street, a jittery snake of anticipation.

Dennis, ever the opportunist, decided to "queue-jump" by pretending he'd been saving a spot for someone. The someone, of course, didn't exist.

"Oi, back of the line!" shouted Moira, who'd been standing there long enough to develop a frostbite tan.

"I was here ages ago," Dennis argued, clutching his stomach theatrically. "Left to find a loo. You wouldn't deny a man his dignity, would you?"

"Your dignity left with your last sandwich," Moira shot back.

The argument spiralled into a full-blown debate over queue ethics, complete with witnesses and a self-appointed referee. By the time it was settled, the shepherd's pie was gone, replaced with something the volunteers vaguely called "vegetable casserole." Dennis sulked all night, claiming the world had conspired against him.

The Public Toilet Tango

Public toilets were another battleground, marked by invisible "members-only" signs we could never access. They were open to the public, sure, but not to our public. The moment we walked in, the looks began—the tightening of mouths, the raised eyebrows, the shuffle of handbags clutched tighter.

I remember one afternoon, ducking into a station toilet, only to be stopped by an attendant who looked me up and down like I'd just crawled out of a bin (I had, but that's beside the point).

"Fifty pence," she said firmly.

I handed over the last of my change, and she hesitated before letting me through. Her face said it all: You don't belong here.

Inside, I washed my hands twice, more out of spite than cleanliness. As I left, she called after me, "Try the café next time. They're... more your type."

Her words lingered long after I'd walked away. It wasn't just access to toilets we were denied—it was access to basic humanity.

The Lasagne That Wasn't

Occasionally, rumours of a "good meal" spread like wildfire, sparking a desperate scramble to get there first. One memorable night, the talk was of lasagne at St. Anne's—a holy grail of street cuisine if ever there was one. Carl was beside himself.

"Proper layers, Bob," he said, practically dragging me along. "Not that soggy mush they call lasagne at some places."

We arrived to find a queue so long it looked like a festival line-up. Spirits were high, though. People joked about how far they'd come for this mythical lasagne, some claiming to have hitchhiked, others swearing they'd sold their last pair of socks for a bus ticket.

When the trays finally emerged, a hush fell over the crowd. The smell was intoxicating—cheesy, savoury, promising comfort. But as the first plates were handed out, reality hit. The "lasagne" was a single sheet of pasta topped with what could generously be called bolognese sauce. Carl stared at his plate, crestfallen.

"They promised layers," he whispered.

Moira took a bite and shrugged. "Well, it's got a layer, singular. That counts, right?"

Carl's devastation became the running joke for weeks. Every time someone mentioned food, someone else would mutter, "At least it's got layers," sending us all into fits of laughter.

The Invisible Hierarchy

Even among the homeless, there were unspoken rules about who "deserved" what. Certain spots were unofficially reserved for long-timers. Certain queues had pecking orders. And certain people—like Phil, with his endless charm—seemed to get the best of everything.

One morning, a new bloke arrived at the Salvation Army, his face weathered but unfamiliar. He eyed the group warily before asking where to queue for food.

"No queue today," Phil said, patting the seat beside him. "You're sitting with the VIPs."

The man looked confused but sat anyway. By the end of the meal, Phil had not only shared his bread roll but convinced the volunteers to give him an extra blanket.

"Phil's got the gift of the gab," I whispered to Carl. "He could sell snow to a penguin."

"Or lasagne to you," Carl quipped.

The Rationed Kindness of Society

Kindness on the streets was rationed like food—dished out sparingly and often with strings attached. The sandwich van was a rare exception, turning up every Thursday with no judgment and plenty of tea. One week, it didn't arrive. Panic set in almost immediately.

"What happened?" Moira demanded, as if the van had personally betrayed her.

"Heard it broke down," Dennis said solemnly. "Tragic, really."

The rumour mill churned out increasingly dramatic theories—everything from sabotage to a government plot. By evening, we'd decided to stage a rescue mission. Phil led the charge, brandishing a makeshift sign that read Save the Sandwiches!

The following week, the van returned, and the driver was greeted like a war hero. Someone even sang "For He's a Jolly Good Fellow." The sandwiches tasted better than ever, though that might've been the relief talking.

The Humour That Held Us Together

Humour wasn't just a coping mechanism—it was survival. It turned indignities into anecdotes, failures into farces. Like the time Carl tried to invent a "street stove" using a biscuit tin and a candle. It worked for about two minutes before the tin caught fire.

"Look, lads!" Carl shouted, holding up the flaming tin. "Hot food, faster than Deliveroo!"

Then there was Dennis, who decided to build his own "portable shelter" out of tarps and duct tape. A gust of wind turned it into a sail, dragging him halfway down the street.

"I'm flying, lads!" he yelled, clutching the flapping tarp like it was the mast of a pirate ship.

The Lines That Really Mattered

For all the queues, toilets, and makeshift stoves, the most important lines were the ones we drew for ourselves. They were the boundaries between giving up and holding on, between surviving and truly living. Some days, those lines felt impossibly thin.

"You think anyone sees us?" Moira asked one night, staring at the stars.

"Sometimes," I said. "Enough to keep going."

And that was the truth. For every closed door, every cold night, there was a moment—a smile from a stranger, a warm cup of tea, a shared laugh—that reminded us we were still human.

Life on the streets wasn't just about staying warm or fed; it was about navigating those invisible lines without losing yourself. We laughed, we struggled, and we kept going—not because it was easy, but because it was the only choice we had.

As Carl said one morning, raising his chipped mug in a mock toast, "Still here, Bob. That's gotta count for something."

"It does," I replied. "It counts for everything."

And in that moment, it really did.

Chapter Eleven:

Friendships Forged in the Shadows

Homelessness wasn't just about survival. It was about connections—sometimes fleeting, sometimes deep, but always unique. Friendships on the streets weren't like the ones I'd had in my old life. They were forged in the harshest conditions, shaped by shared struggles, and often sprinkled with an unexpected dose of humour. These bonds were as vital as food or shelter, carrying us through the darkest nights and the coldest mornings.

This chapter is about those friendships, the characters who coloured my days, and the ways we found to hold each other up—sometimes literally.

The Arrival of Maggie

One morning, as I shuffled into our usual spot by the bus station, I noticed someone new. She was sitting cross-legged on the pavement, wearing mismatched socks and a bright pink hat that looked like it had been knitted by an enthusiastic but distracted child. She was humming a tune I couldn't place, completely unfazed by the chaos around her.

"That's Maggie," Carl said, nodding towards her. "Bit of an odd one, but harmless."

Maggie turned out to be a whirlwind of energy. Within days, she'd established herself as the group's unofficial "entertainment director." Armed with a battered harmonica and an endless supply of stories, she became a beacon of light in our little community.

One evening, as the sun dipped below the rooftops, Maggie organised an impromptu "talent show." Phil sang a wildly off-key rendition of Hey Jude, Dennis performed what he called "shadow puppetry for the sophisticated," and Carl recited a gardening poem so heartfelt it brought a tear to Moira's eye.

When it was Maggie's turn, she stood up, harmonica in hand, and announced, "This is called the 'Pigeon Blues.'" She launched into a tune so chaotic it sounded like she was wrestling the harmonica rather than playing it. By the end, we were all in stitches.

"Encore!" Dennis shouted, clapping wildly.

"Careful what you wish for," Maggie replied, winking.

The 'Great Blanket Heist'

Maggie wasn't just funny—she was resourceful. One particularly cold night, she came up with a plan to raid a charity drop-off point that had been locked inside a churchyard. Technically, it wasn't stealing, she reasoned. The blankets were meant for us, and we were just speeding up the distribution process.

With Maggie as our ringleader, we executed what could only be described as the least covert heist in history. Armed with a bent coat hanger and an old mop handle, we spent twenty minutes trying to hook a blanket through the iron gate while whispering loudly enough to wake the neighbourhood.

"Quiet!" Maggie hissed, jabbing Dennis with the mop handle. "You'll scare the pigeons."

"We're not the noisy ones," Carl muttered, gesturing to Maggie's bright pink hat.

We finally retrieved three blankets, only to find that one was covered in moth holes. Maggie shrugged. "Character-building," she said, draping it over her shoulders like a cape.

Carl's Gardening School

Carl, ever the optimist, decided to start a "gardening school" for the group. Using a patch of overgrown weeds by the park, he held lessons on everything from soil health to pruning techniques. None of us had a garden, but that didn't stop Carl.

"Gardening's not about the space," he declared one morning. "It's about the mindset."

Phil raised an eyebrow. "And what mindset goes with nettles?"

"Survival," Carl shot back. "Same as us."

Despite the absurdity, Carl's lessons became a regular event. He taught us how to spot edible plants, how to make compost from scraps, and how to "grow hope" even in the bleakest conditions.

One day, Moira found a half-crushed flowerpot and proudly presented it to Carl. "Your first student project," she said with a rare smile.

Carl beamed. "We'll plant something beautiful. Maybe daisies."

"Or weeds," Phil added. "Stick to what we're good at."

The Day Dennis Got Philosophical

Dennis was the group's resident conspiracy theorist, but every now and then, he'd surprise us with moments of startling wisdom. One evening, as we huddled around a shared flask of tea, he leaned back and sighed.

"Funny thing about this life," he said. "It strips away all the nonsense. You find out what really matters."

"And what's that?" Moira asked, sceptical.

Dennis gestured around the group. "This. Us. Laughing at pigeons and nicking blankets. It's not much, but it's real."

For a moment, there was silence. Then Maggie broke it with a loud, exaggerated sniff. "Alright, who gave Dennis feelings?"

We all laughed, but his words stuck with me. Life on the streets had a way of cutting through the noise, leaving behind the raw, unvarnished truth. And the truth was, we needed each other.

The 'Luxury' Feast

One of my favourite memories was the day we threw what we called a "luxury feast." It started when Phil found an unopened pack of biscuits and Maggie acquired a tin of peaches from a kind passer-by. We pooled our resources, scrounging together everything from slightly squashed bananas to a half-eaten sandwich Carl had saved "just in case."

Maggie, of course, took charge. "We'll need a centrepiece," she announced, arranging the biscuits in a precarious pyramid. "And a theme. I'm thinking... tropical chic."

"Tropical?" Moira said, raising an eyebrow. "We've got bananas and rain. That's about it."

Despite the limited ingredients, the feast was a triumph. We sat under a railway bridge, toasting each other with paper cups of tea and declaring it the finest meal we'd ever had.

"I feel posh," Dennis said, nibbling on a biscuit. "Like I should be wearing a bow tie."

Carl grinned. "I'd settle for a clean shirt."

The Bonds That Kept Us Going

For all the laughter and absurdity, the friendships we built were what kept us going. They were messy, imperfect, and sometimes fleeting, but they were real. On the hardest days, when the cold bit through every layer and hope felt like a distant memory, it was the people around me who made survival possible.

Maggie's harmonica, Carl's gardening lessons, Dennis's wild theories—these were more than distractions. They were lifelines. They reminded us that even in the darkest corners, there was still light to be found.

The Reality Beneath the Jokes

Beneath the humour, though, was the harsh reality of our situation. We laughed because we had to. We made jokes because the alternative was despair. But the truth was, every one of us carried wounds that couldn't be seen. We'd all lost something—homes, families, futures—and we were fighting to hold onto what little we had left.

"You think this'll ever change?" I asked Carl one night as we stared up at the stars.

"Maybe," he said. "Maybe not. But as long as we're still laughing, Bob, we've got a chance."

When I set out to write Homeless But Not Hopeless, I knew it wasn't going to be just my story. This is a fictional account, carefully crafted to protect the dignity and privacy of those who are still living this reality. While the characters and events are inspired by true experiences, they represent a broader truth about life on the streets—a world I was fortunate to leave behind, but one I can never truly forget.

I am one step above homeless now, lucky to have found some stability. Yet, every cold day and night, I think of those still out there, battling the elements, navigating the chaos, and finding ways to survive. Their struggles are no less real because of their invisibility, and their resilience deserves recognition.

This book is as much about humour as it is about hardship. In the darkest moments, laughter became my salvation. It wasn't just a way to cope; it was a way to connect, to remind myself and those around me that we were still human. Whether it was Carl turning weeds into gardening lessons, Phil hosting a "luxury feast" with stale bread, or Dennis waging war on pigeons, these moments of absurdity gave us hope. They proved that even when life takes everything, it cannot take away our ability to laugh.

But I also wrote this book to highlight the systemic failures that leave so many without a safety net. The broken queues, the endless forms, and the well-meaning but disjointed efforts of charities and services are a reminder that more needs to be done. For every act of kindness that kept us going, there were cracks in the system that let too many slip through.

I hope this story serves as a bridge between worlds. For those who have never faced homelessness, I hope it opens your eyes to the reality of life on the streets—the humour, the heartache, and the humanity. And for those still living it, I hope it offers a moment of solidarity, a reminder that you are not alone, and that even in the hardest times, there is light to be found.

Writing this book has been a journey of reflection and gratitude. I am grateful to those who showed me kindness when I needed it most, and to the people whose resilience inspired these pages. Life has moved me on, but it has not let me forget. The bench, the cold nights, and the laughter shared in unlikely places will always stay with me.

To those still out there, this story is for you. May it remind us all of the power of humour, hope, and human connection—even when the world feels at its coldest.

Thank you for your time and support.

Acknowledgements

Writing *Homeless But Not Hopeless* has been an emotional and transformative journey, and it would not have been possible without the inspiration and support of so many incredible people.

To Carl, my steadfast companion on the streets, whose humour, wisdom, and resilience gave me hope when I needed it most—this book owes much of its heart to you.

To everyone at the Salvation Army, your warmth, kindness, and tireless efforts to help those in need were a lifeline. Thank you for showing the world what true compassion looks like.

To my friends lost in Ukraine and to Inessa and the incredible friends I met in Krakow—you've taught me the value of courage, connection, and love in the face of adversity.

To Deborah from GMP, your unwavering support over 40 years and belief in me during some of my darkest moments has left an indelible mark on my life.

To Kelly from Cheshire West, thank you for your persistence, care, and determination to make a difference within a challenging system.

To the countless doctors and psychologists who helped me face my challenges with PTSD, Parkinson's, and beyond—your dedication to healing minds and bodies is a gift I'll forever be grateful for.

To Dave, my amazing brother, thank you for being my rock and for standing by me through every twist and turn. Your support has meant more than words can express.

To my friends at Kings Church in Frodsham thank you for baptising me and opening doors that others had closed on me.

Finally, profound gratitude to those I've spent my life with before this chapter began. Whether through joy, heartbreak, or growth, you've all shaped the person I am today.

This book is a testament to all of you—the people who gave me strength, laughter, and a reason to hope. Thank you for inspiring me to tell this story.

Disclaimer

Homeless But Not Hopeless is a work of fiction inspired by real experiences. While many events and scenarios depicted in this book reflect the realities of homelessness, all characters, names, and specific situations are entirely fictional and have been created to protect the privacy and dignity of individuals who may still be living through these challenges.

Any resemblance to actual persons, living or deceased, or real-life events is purely coincidental. This book is intended to highlight the resilience, humour, and humanity of those navigating homelessness while raising awareness of the systemic and social issues they face.

The author has taken care to ensure the content is respectful and sensitive, aiming to provide a voice for the voiceless and inspire understanding and empathy.

Printed in Great Britain
by Amazon